Visiting the Past

Mesa Verde

Jane Shuter

Heinemann Library
Chicago, Illinois

Published by Heinemann Library,
an imprint of Reed Educational & Professional Publishing,
100 N. LaSalle, Suite 1010
Chicago, Illinois 60602

Customer Service 1-888-454-2279

Designed by Lisa Buckley
Illustrations by Gerald Wood
Photographs by Tristan Boyer
Printed in Hong Kong

04 03 02 01 00
10 9 8 7 6 5 4 3 2 1

Library of Congress Cataloging-In-Publication Data

Shuter, Jane.
    Mesa Verde / Jane Shuter
        p. cm. -- (Visiting the past)
    Includes bibliographical references and index
    Summary: Discusses the cliff dwellings of Mesa Verde, Colorado,
and what is known about the history, social life, and customs of the
Ancestral Puebloans who lived in them.
    ISBN 1-57572-858-3 (lib. bdg.)
    1. Mesa Verde National Park (Colo.)--Juvenile literature.
2. Pueblo Indians--Antiquities--Juvenile literature. 3. Pueblo
Indians--Social life and customs--Juvenile literature. 4. Cliff
-dwellings--Colorado--Juvenile literature. 5. Colorado-
-Antiquities--Juvenile literature. [1. Pueblo Indians. 2. Indians
of North America--Colorado. 3. Mesa Verde National Park (Colo.).
4. National parks and reserves. 5. Colorado--Antiquities.]
I. Title. II. Series.
E99.P9S53 1999   99-17395
978.8'27--dc21   CIP

Acknowledgments
With many thanks to all those at Mesa Verde National Park who gave unstintingly of their time to this project. Especial thanks to Rangers Jim Atkinson and Clyde Benally and to curators Gian Mercurio and Donna J. Read, who changed a lot of my preconceptions and made this a better book.

Any words appearing in the text in bold, **like this**, are explained in the Glossary.

Contents

Early People of Mesa Verde

The cliff dwellings of Mesa Verde, Colorado, thrill thousands of visitors every year. People are full of questions: Who lived there? Where did they come from? Why did they live in **alcoves** in the cliffs? How did they live? Why did they leave and where did they go?

We know that people lived in these cliff dwellings more than 700 years ago, but they left no written records. We do not even know what they called themselves. **Archaeologists** and historians have had to guess the answers. They use evidence from the sites and the lifestyles of living Puebloan people. These people are descendants of the people who we call Ancestral Puebloans, who once lived at Mesa Verde. Cliff Palace and Spruce Tree House are the sites visited in this book.

Archaeologists removed samples of wood, which were replaced with corks, from these wooden beams. They counted the rings that show each year of tree growth to calculate when the wood was cut.

Posts and doorways show different floor levels and where balconies ran along the outside walls. Rectangular and T-shaped spaces were both doors.

Black smoke stains show where fires were lit regularly.

Trash piles at Cliff Palace and Spruce Tree House provide archaeologists with evidence about what people wore, made, and ate, and what they farmed and what tools they used.

These hollows in the soft sandstone show where the Ancestral Puebloans sharpened their hard stone axes.

These circular buildings, all built in a similar design, clearly had a special function.

At first, Mesa Verde may look like a difficult place to farm, with its steep **canyons** and scarcity of water. However, the **mesa** topsoil is **fertile** enough for a variety of plants to grow.

The first people to settle on Mesa Verde for any length of time arrived in about A.D. 500. **Nomadic** people had been there before, mostly on hunting expeditions. The settlers found many wild animals, water, fertile soil, and trees for firewood on the mesa tops. It was a good place to live. They settled here in groups, living in pit houses. These were half below and half above the ground, and roofed with a wooden frame covered with a thick layer of **adobe**. The settlers had chosen well. They found that Mesa Verde had one of the longest growing seasons in the area.

More people came to live on the mesas. They stayed and had families, so the population grew and grew. They began to make pottery, which gave them better storage and cooking pots than the baskets they had previously used. This pottery helped them cook more food in different ways. People began to grow squash, corn, and beans, and raise turkeys for a constant supply of feathers and meat.

5

Living in the Cliffs

In about 1150, the Ancestral Puebloans began to move down from the **mesa** top into the **alcoves** in the sandstone cliffs. These alcoves were formed by water seeping down into the cliff, freezing in cold weather, and expanding. This expansion caused the sandstone to crack, flake, and fall away. Over thousands of years, the small gaps in the cliff face grew to become alcoves big enough for people to make their homes inside. Many of the alcoves were small, so the dwellings in them were small, too. Of the 600 or so cliff dwellings in Mesa Verde National Park, 77 percent of them are tucked into small alcoves that held 1 to 5 rooms. People may have used the smallest alcoves just for storage instead of dwellings.

The spring at the Spruce Tree House settlement was one reason for choosing to build there. One can see how seeping water has caused the stone to flake and crack. Many pieces have fallen on the ground below. Seeping water collected in the area to the left of the photograph. The amount of water there varied with the seasons.

Why did the Ancestral Puebloans move into these alcoves? There are several possible reasons. The climate was changing and getting colder. The alcoves gave more shelter. Most cliff dwellings face south or southwest to receive more winter sunlight and to provide shelter from the cold northern winds. Moving also freed more land for farming to feed everyone. The population was growing. More people tried to grow enough to eat on small areas of land that were used over and over and had become less **fertile**. There is evidence that the farmers switched crops around so that the same crops did not take the same nutrients from the ground every year. They also allowed land to rest from time to time. Even so, they may not have been able to keep the soil as fertile.

Some historians suggest that the move down to the alcoves was defensive—either because groups were fighting among themselves for food or groups responded to an outside threat. There is little evidence to support this theory. It is much more likely that they moved in a carefully worked out response to changes in their living conditions.

An artist's drawing of what the Spruce Tree House settlement may have looked like in about 1270. About 150 people lived there at this time, making it the third largest settlement of the cliff dwellings.

Skilled Builders

The cliff dwellings were built with great skill and care. This was a huge task for the Ancestral Puebloans, who had only stone tools and no machinery. They used the same basic techniques with variations. **Archaeologists** are beginning to identify the work of individual masons. The builders worked with materials that were available and built to fit the shape of the **alcove**. Sometimes they worked around large boulders that were too difficult to clear.

At least some of the buildings went up to fit into the roof of the alcove.

The buildings go into the back of the alcove. Builders built rooms at the back of the alcove first and then worked forward.

This photograph of the Cliff Palace settlement shows the skill of the builders.

Builders worked around the remaining boulders that were too difficult to break up and move.

The remains of black and pink **plaster** show that the builders decorated some buildings inside and outside.

8

Building techniques

These photographs of walls from Cliff Palace and Spruce Tree House show the various techniques of wall building. The builders chipped the large stones into shape with stone axes and fastened them together with **adobe** mortar. The mortar was not very strong, so they often pushed smaller stones into the mortar to make it stronger. Archaeologists call this "chinking."

Buildings were carefully plastered. Sometimes builders had to put a mud layer over a bumpy stone surface to make it smooth enough to plaster.

The "pecking" marks on these stones were part of the finishing process.

Doorways were either rectangular or T-shaped. The smaller holes probably provided more light and air.

The Ancestral Puebloans decorated some inside walls by painting designs on the plaster.

The builders made upper floors by laying large beams across the building. Then they laid smaller poles, which ran the other way, across the beams. They placed sticks or bark on top and finished with a layer of adobe about six inches thick.

This "dry walling" was done without using mortar. Maybe the builders had to do an emergency repair or it was a dry time of year when there was no water to spare for mortar.

Houses and Homes

How did the Ancestral Puebloans use these buildings? **Archaeologists** cannot be completely sure. However, it seems that the basic rooms, which were only about 6 feet by 8 feet (2 meters by 3 meters) and 5.5 feet (1.5 meters) high, were used mainly as sleeping rooms and maybe places to work during bad weather. Some, but not all, of these rooms have **hearths** for fires. Some rooms also have small holes in the walls that would have allowed more light.

People probably did most of their work outside together. The women ground corn, made pottery and baskets, and cooked. The men made tools and wove cloth. Men and women made turkey feather blankets or clothes. The children and older people helped or talked and played. They fed the turkeys and kept animals out of the crops.

In a corner of this room, one can see a fire pit and the smoke stains from many fires on the wall behind it.

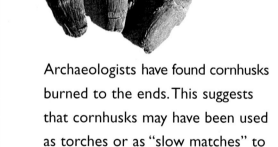

Archaeologists have found cornhusks burned to the ends. This suggests that cornhusks may have been used as torches or as "slow matches" to carry fire from one place to another.

This gives a good idea of the size of a room. The doorway in the back is blocked with a stone. Stones were used as doors in winter; mats or woven cloth were used in summer. Sometimes storerooms were sealed off with a stone to keep the contents safe and dry. Sometimes, perhaps in bad winters, people who died were buried in sealed off storerooms.

Family life

How did families organize themselves? Many Puebloans today say that their culture has always been based on groups with shared female ancestors. The Ancestral Puebloans probably lived in this way. Several groups of people with the same female ancestor may have lived in a series of rooms and shared a kiva. Kivas were special circular, roofed structures that were used as winter work places and for gatherings and religious ceremonies. There were several groups with the same female ancestor in larger cliff dwellings.

People probably did most of their work in the biggest front courtyard at the Spruce Tree House settlement, especially during good weather. It also had easy access to the two kivas built underneath the courtyard.

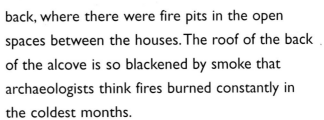

The balcony ran across the front of this building. Some of the flooring on the left and its supports are still in place on either side. People sat out on these balconies to work or talk. You can also see the changes in the stonework showing that the building was altered at least once.

In winter, people probably spent less time in the more exposed courtyards. They moved into kivas or toward the back, where there were fire pits in the open spaces between the houses. The roof of the back of the alcove is so blackened by smoke that archaeologists think fires burned constantly in the coldest months.

11

What Were Kivas?

Kivas are easily recognized. They are the circular buildings that are underground. In most cases, the only way in or out was by ladder through the roof. The Ancestral Puebloans probably used kivas in several ways. They were used for religious ceremonies. At other times, they were used for family gatherings, as a place for visitors to stay, and as a work place in winter. Some kivas have marks on the floor showing that weaving looms were fastened there.

Not all kivas look exactly the same. Some kivas were connected to each other or to other rooms by tunnels. **Archaeologists** wonder if people used different kivas in different ways—some as family spaces and others for larger group meetings and ceremonies.

Air came into the kiva through this ventilation shaft.

The air then hit the deflector stone, which moved it evenly around the kiva and pushed the warmer, smoky air up through the entrance.

A fire was lit in this fire pit.

The roof beams sat on top of these six pillars.

These are shelves, not benches.

About half of the kivas on Mesa Verde have one of these small holes called a sipapu. For living Puebloans, they are the link that allowed the spirits of all things to enter the physical world.

The large ventilation hole in the center of this courtyard in Spruce Tree House provides air for one of the kivas under this courtyard. The ladders show the kiva entrances.

The ladder usually came into the kiva between the fire pit and the sipapu. People may have thrown special herbs on the fire during religious ceremonies so that people entering and leaving the kiva passed through the **purifying** smoke.

The National Park Service reconstructed this kiva at Spruce Tree House by using techniques and materials similar to those of the Ancestral Puebloans. This photo was taken when there was full sunlight above ground. This is the most natural light a kiva would have had, although there was also light from the fire and possibly cornhusk torches.

Beliefs

Physical evidence survives of what Ancestral Puebloans wore and ate, but there is no physical evidence about their beliefs. It is clear they believed in an afterlife. They buried their dead with things to use in that afterlife, as have many other civilizations. They buried people on the **mesa** top and in **canyons**. They also buried people in the same careful way— in **alcoves**, trash piles, and blocked rooms. It is possible that these were winter burials because they are places that would have been easy to reach even in the worst weather.

This kiva in Cliff Palace has a tunnel that leads to a small back room. Living Puebloans suggest that this may have been used as a dramatic entrance in a religious ceremony.

Almost all of our ideas about Ancestral Puebloan beliefs are based on the ways of living Puebloans who preserve the traditions of their people with great care. They use kivas so they can explain how the Ancestral Puebloans may have used them. They believe all living things have a physical self and a spirit self. Many things about the Ancestral Puebloans suggest they had similar beliefs to those of living Puebloans. For example, a sipapu was an entrance to the physical world from the spirit world. Living Puebloan beliefs support the idea that the Ancestral Puebloans believed in nature spirits. Many groups of people who depend on farming for a living develop beliefs in nature spirits. This is as true today as it was in the time of the Ancestral Puebloans or the ancient Egyptians.

14

Studying the sky

Many people think the Ancestral Puebloans studied the sun, moon, and stars and that many ceremonies were linked to the way things lined up in the sky. Changes in the weather and studying the sky would have helped them to decide when to plant or harvest crops. Some of the larger settlements might have been divided into two distinct groups. These groups possibly organized the various winter and summer ceremonies.

The walls on either side of this passageway may have divided the "winter people" from the "summer people," who were responsible for winter and summer ceremonies in Spruce Tree House. There is a similar division in Cliff Palace.

Many walls were decorated with bands of white and pink **plaster**. Some living Puebloans use this decoration style in similar styles in their cultures, which show the division between "Father Sky" and "Mother Earth."

Clothes

The climate at Mesa Verde is both extremely hot and very cold. The Ancestral Puebloans wore different clothes in different seasons. In summer, the women wore woven cotton blankets draped over one shoulder or belted to make a dress. In the hottest weather, they wore simple aprons made from cotton and yucca fiber. Men wore cotton tunics or in hot weather, they wore loincloths. Everyday clothes were probably made from plain cloth, but the Ancestral Puebloan weavers also made beautifully patterned and dyed cloth for special clothing. Everyone wore light sandals made from yucca leaf fiber. The texture of sandals and clothes made from yucca varied depending on whether they used whole or split leaves, thin leaf fiber, or crushed and matted leaf fiber.

In winter, the Ancestral Puebloans wore robes and blankets made of turkey feathers and turkey feather socks inside their sandals or turkey feather boots. **Archaeologists** have found pieces of animal hide cut into shapes and sewn together with yucca twine, which may have been used for clothing. Babies spent most of their time in cradles stuffed with juniper bark as a kind of diaper. When they grew old enough to walk, children probably wore the same kind of clothes as adults, although many infants and small children wore rabbit skin robes in winter instead of turkey feathers.

The yucca plant was vital for more than clothing. People also made cord, snares, baskets, thread, mats, and even paintbrushes from the fiber of the leaves. They made needles from the spiky leaf tips. They ate the flowers in spring and the fruit in fall. The sap from the roots made a liquid soap. The tree behind the yucca, which is shedding its bark, is a juniper tree.

Winter and summer wear

This tightly braided and knotted woman's summer apron was made from fine yucca fiber and cotton that may have been grown on the mesa top or brought back by traders. The fringes were originally longer.

This child's summer sandal has a strong protective ridge at the toe end, shaped for the big toe. The fastenings are gone, but they may have been yucca cords that attached to either side of the sandal where there is fraying. Summer sandals were made in various styles, but all of them had strong bottoms and yucca cord ties that left most of the foot bare.

This winter sock was made from yucca fiber and turkey feathers and was probably worn inside a sandal.

This small pouch was made from matted yucca fibers stitched together and decorated with yucca cord thread.

Food and Cooking

The Ancestral Puebloans ate a variety of wild and farm animals and plants. **Archaeologists** mostly know what they ate from studying what they threw away, including **excrement**. Corn cobs, other foods including cactus seeds, and animal bones have been found in trash piles.

The Ancestral Puebloans hunted wild rabbits, deer, and other animals on the **mesa** tops. They farmed turkeys mainly for their feathers but also for meat. Farmers grew corn, squash, and beans. Berries, piñon nuts, acorns, and the leaves of wild herbs such as sage were used to flavor food, as was salt brought by **traders**. Many herbs were used as medicine and in herbal teas.

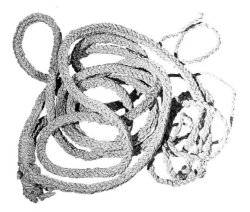

This snare was made from braided yucca cord. It would have taken a long time to make, but the complicated braiding system made the cord very strong.

Cooks often roasted the purplish cactus fruit and used the juniper berries (on the tree behind the cactus) to flavor other food.

People chewed the pine sap as a form of chewing gum.

Piñon pine nuts were a good source of food. The nuts could be roasted, boiled, or eaten raw.

18

Cooking

How did the Ancestral Puebloans cook their food? We do not have exact recipes, but we can guess from their cooking pots and facilities. They had big cooking pots to cook food over a fire. There is no evidence of specially built ovens, only open fires for cooking. They would probably have roasted different kinds of food, including meat and cactus, over a fire on long **skewers**. They stored much of their food whole, like corn, berries, and nuts, and they may have dried meat for long-term storage.

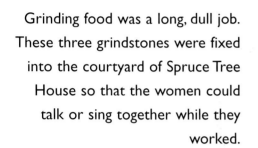

Grinding food was a long, dull job. These three grindstones were fixed into the courtyard of Spruce Tree House so that the women could talk or sing together while they worked.

This cooking pot was originally the same color inside and outside. The smoke from countless cooking fires has blackened the outside.

Farming

Mesa Verde has very little rain, yet the Ancestral Puebloans were farmers. How did they manage to grow crops in a place with such a shortage of water? Sometimes they didn't. **Archaeologists** examined yearly tree growth and found that there were several years of severe **drought** when most of the crops planted by the Ancestral Puebloans would have failed. When this occurred, the Ancestral Puebloans had to rely on food stored from previous years. However, most of the time the Ancestral Puebloans farmed very successfully. They used **dry farming** techniques including planting deep into the soil where most moisture could be found and building **terraces** to trap water. **Silt** washed down by occasional heavy rains produced very **fertile** soil. Farmers also tried to conserve as much water as possible in **reservoirs**.

The Ancestral Puebloans built farming terraces like these to trap any water and silt that was running downhill.

The farmers probably noticed that using the same land over and over made it less fertile. This is the kind of land they had to clear to make new areas to farm.

The Ancestral Puebloans farmed as much of the mesa top as they could. However, they did not farm close to the cliff edge where soil was easily washed or blown away, which left bare sandstone. Any soil close to the edge could lose nutrients. Minerals in the soil that seeped over the top made the black stains.

The Ancestral Puebloans grew corn, squash, and beans. They saved corn from one year as seed for the next. By choosing the seed corn carefully, they bred different types of corn. Archaeologists have found many types of corn in trash piles with four to twenty rows on each ear. The Ancestral Puebloans also bred beans and squash. They farmed turkeys, some of which they kept in pens in cliff dwellings for part of the year. At other times, turkeys roamed the **mesa** top. The children probably had the job of keeping turkeys and other animals away from the crops.

The Ancestral Puebloans used digging sticks like these to farm the land.

The farmers grew different varieties of corn. They chose the seed to plant the next year from cobs that grew best in dry climate.

These Merriam's turkeys are a modern breed similar to those the Ancestral Puebloans farmed. They live wild on the mesa top.

Cliff Palace

Archaeologists gave Cliff Palace its name because of its size. It is the largest of all the cliff dwellings on the **mesa**. Cliff Palace had about 150 rooms. This means about 200 people could have lived here—depending on how many of the structures went all the way to the top of the alcove and how many stopped at the second story.

Cliff Palace is noticeable even from across the mesa. Close up, it is huge.

More than just a home?

Some people think that, while Cliff Palace had some permanent inhabitants, it may also have been a place where people from all over the mesa, maybe even from further away, met to trade, arrange marriages, and attend special religious ceremonies. Cliff Palace could have been an administrative center for Mesa Verde, but we do not know if all cliff dwellers saw themselves as a single people, or even spoke the same language. Some people think surplus corn grown on the mesa was collected at Cliff Palace and traded to settlements further south, where the growing season was not as good. There is no archaeological evidence for this, but we do know the cliff dwellers traded with each other and with other groups.

Most of the rooms in this upper ledge were storage rooms for food, which was mainly corn. When full, the storerooms probably held enough corn to feed not only the inhabitants of Cliff Palace, but also other local groups in times of **drought** and crop failure.

This door was the only way into the storage rooms.

This storage wall was repaired without **mortar,** perhaps at a time when water for mixing was in short supply.

Mesa Verde and the Wider World

There is plenty of evidence that the Ancestral Puebloans traded with other people. **Artifacts** have been found from as far away as the Pacific Coast, although this does not mean the Ancestral Puebloans traveled that far. Maybe they had contact with someone who had traveled there. There was certainly a lot of local trade. The Ancestral Puebloans traded some things that were vital to their existence, such as hard stone to make their tools. Other things like shells and pottery had **scarcity value**.

Everything they traded had to be carried. Some people believe they have traced trade routes that passed by areas that had water for travelers. The map below shows where the goods found at Mesa Verde came from and the things Ancestral Puebloans may have taken and brought back from trading trips.

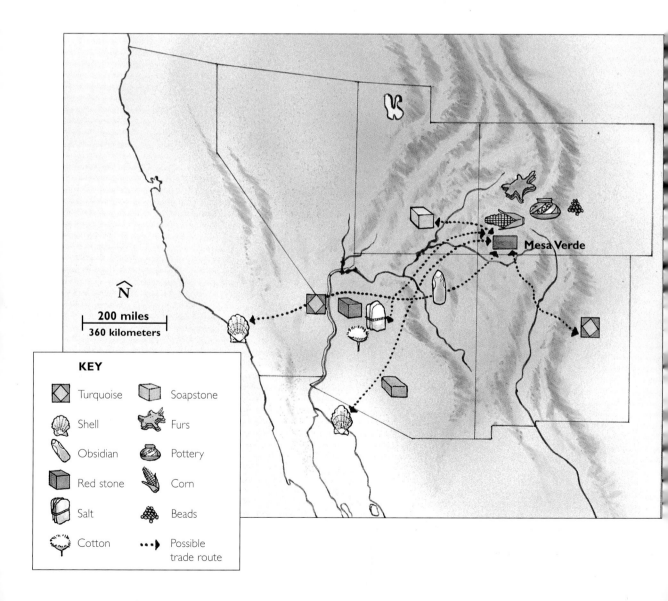

Mesa Verde

N

200 miles
360 kilometers

KEY

Turquoise		Soapstone	
Shell		Furs	
Obsidian		Pottery	
Red stone		Corn	
Salt		Beads	
Cotton		Possible trade route	

Goods brought back to Mesa Verde

This stone arrowhead was made from a piece of stone that came from Utah, as did the piece beside it.

This ax head was made from stone from the Mancos River area. It would have had a wooden handle, which was fastened securely with yucca fiber cord.

Goods traded from Mesa Verde

The Ancestral Puebloans also probably traded **surplus** food they could not eat or store, although they would not often have such a surplus. Piñon nuts were valuable and easy to carry in large quantities.

The Ancestral Puebloans probably traded good examples of their black and white pottery, like this mug and pot for holding corn. They would not have traded ordinary pottery, such as cooking pots and bowls.

Why Did They Go?

From about 1280 through the next fifteen years, the Ancestral Puebloans moved from the cliff dwellings of Mesa Verde. They headed south and built new communities. Why did they go?

• Some people say the climate drove them away. Certainly the growing season became shorter and the winters became colder. There was a series of longer **droughts** from 1276 to 1297. These reasons, plus overworked soil that was less and less **fertile,** meant farming was more difficult.

• Other people suggest that the steadily increasing population reached a point where the Ancestral Puebloans could not feed everyone.

• People who see the cliff dwellings as defensive structures suggest the Ancestral Puebloans were driven out of Mesa Verde by enemies, but there is no evidence of others using the **mesa** sites after them.

• Other people consider the move as part of a larger, planned **migration** that stretched over many generations and was tied to religion. The original settlement of Mesa Verde may have been part of this move, and some religious ceremonies may have passed on knowledge about the signs that told them to move on.

Probably a combination of all these factors caused the Ancestral Puebloans to leave Mesa Verde. After all, no group of people does things for exactly the same reasons. The climate and population changes could have been some of the signs built into the religious beliefs of the Ancestral Puebloans. Although some people moved mainly for religious reasons, others might have moved just hoping to find an easier life.

Some reminders of the people who moved: a handprint in the plaster of a room in Spruce Tree House; the handholds and footholds that people used to reach the mesa top from Cliff Palace.

After the Ancestral Puebloans

What happened to the cliff dwellings when the Ancestral Puebloans left? The Native Americans knew about the cliff dwellings, so vague rumors about them reached the incoming white settlers. In 1874, members of a government photographic survey team led by William Henry Jackson found and photographed several sites. This led others to hunt for more sites, looking for **artifacts** to sell. In 1891, Gustaf Nordenskiold surveyed the dwellings, using photographs, drawings, and descriptions.

Various groups became concerned about looting and damage to the cliff dwellings and tried to protect the sites. Eventually, in 1906, the government created Mesa Verde National Park. First, the army maintained it. Then, in 1916, the National Park Service was created. Since then, members of the Park Service have tried to keep a balance between preserving the cliff dwellings and letting people visit them. They welcome visitors and provide them with a lot of information, including displays and talks to help them visualize Ancestral Puebloan life. But visitors, even well behaved ones, cause damage just by walking around a site. The National Park Service works to stabilize the sites—that is, maintain them as they are rather than restore them. They restrict access to some sites, including Cliff Palace, which can only be visited on a guided tour.

Using a tour-only system, more than one thousand people pass through Cliff Palace every day.

27

Timeline

500 A.D.	First permanent settlements on Mesa Verde. People live in pithouses, dug out half below ground.
750 A.D.	People start living in larger communities. Pithouses change into above-ground homes and underground kivas.
1150 A.D.	People move from the mesa top into alcoves in the cliffs, like Spruce Tree House and Cliff Palace.
1276-1297 A.D.	A long series of droughts affects Mesa Verde. It becomes harder and harder to raise enough food to feed a growing population.
1278 A.D.	Last evidence of building work on the alcove cliff dwellings.
1280 A.D.	First evidence of people leaving Mesa Verde and moving south.
1292 A.D.	Last evidence of occupation of the alcove cliff dwellings.
1874 A.D.	W.H. Jackson photographs some alcove cliff dwellings as part of a government photograpic survey.
1891 A.D.	First proper survey of the dwellings, by Gustaf Nordenskiold.
1906 A.D.	Mesa Verde National Park set up.
1916 A.D.	National Park Service set up to care for a variety of sites, including Mesa Verde.

Site Maps

Cliff Palace

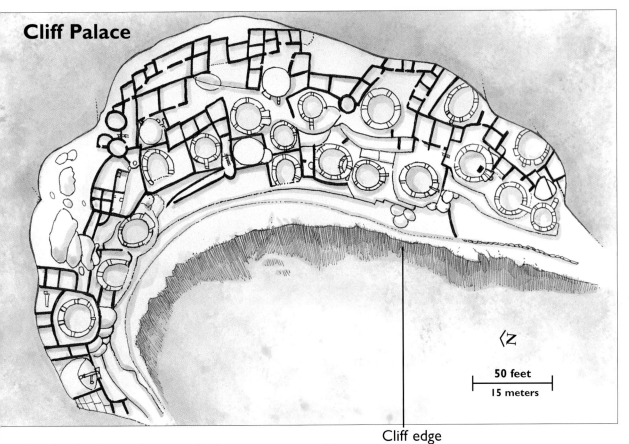

⟨Z

50 feet
15 meters

Cliff edge

On both plans, the rounded structures are kivas.

Spruce Tree House

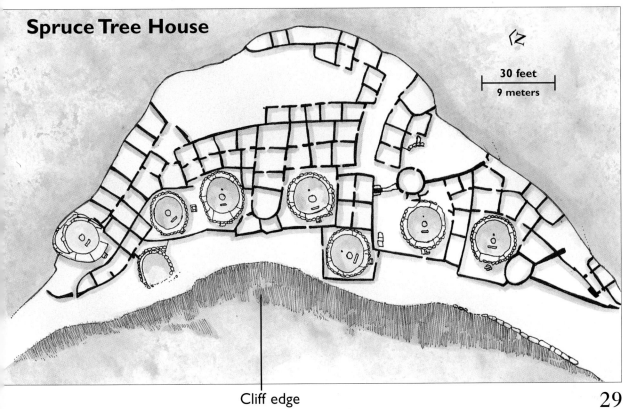

⟨Z

30 feet
9 meters

Cliff edge

Glossary

adobe mixture of clay, ash, and water that can be made into bricks and plaster by shaping and allowing to dry in the sun, or used as mortar while still damp

alcove cave in the side of a cliff, formed when rain water freezes and expands within the rock, causing the sandstone to crack and flake away

archaeologist scientist who investigates the past by examining things that have survived from the past and sometimes digs into the ground to find them

artifact something a person has made, from small things like pins to huge buildings

canyon deep, steep-sided valley

drought time when no rain falls for a long time

dry farming method of farming in a dry climate to make the most of any rain or snow that falls. Farmers plant seeds deeply and raise the soil around the top of each plant to catch any moisture and funnel it to the roots.

excrement solid waste from the human body

fertile to be full of nutrients and able to grow many crops

hearth area in which to light a fire

mesa high, flat area of land

migration moving from one place to another

mortar mixture that is used to join stones, bricks, and other building material together

nomadic moving from one place to another, either to follow animals to hunt them or to move animals so they have fresh grass to eat

plaster something spread over walls or ceilings to produce a smooth surface

purifying cleaning—in this case, a religious cleaning as part of a ceremony (not washing)

reservoir large lake made by people where water is stored

scarcity value something has scarcity value if people want it because there are few objects like it.

silt soil carried along by moving water, such as rain or melting snow

skewers long, thin wooden sticks

surplus something that is left over

terraces areas of land set in a hillside, like a set of steps, that use walls to make flat areas of land that can be farmed

traders people who buy things from one person and sell them to others

*M*ore Books to Read

Hallet, Bill, and Jane Hallet. *Look Up, Look Down, Look all Around Mesa Verde National Park.* Tucson, Ariz.: Look & See Publications, 1990.

Lavender, David. *Mother Earth, Father Sky: The Pueblo Indians of the American Southwest.* New York: Holiday House, Incorporated, 1998.

Martell, Hazel M. *Native Americans & Mesa Verde.* Parsippany, N.J.: Silver Burdett Press, 1993.

Young, Robert. *A Personal Tour of Mesa Verde.* Minneapolis: The Lerner Publishing Group, 1999.

Index